THIS IS MY YEAR

Affirmation Guided Journal

S. Mara

This Is My Year: Affirmation Guided Journal
© 2021 by S. Mara
All rights reserved.

Published by:
Relentless Publishing House, LLC
www.relentlesspublishing.com

ISBN: 978-1-948829-63-2

Welcome!

Use this guided journal to jot down your goals for the next year and beyond. Your "This Is My Year" journal is a safe place to simply express how you feel, document the necessary steps & ACTIONS towards your goals and mark them COMPLETE as you accomplish them. I'll introduce you to SERENITY BREAKS where you will be prompted to freestyle your positive thoughts. Use the TODAY I pages to track your weekly and biweekly progress. I hope this journal is as essential to you as it is to me. After each written expression say out loud "THIS IS MY YEAR".

THIS IS MY YEAR

TODAY YOU'VE TAKEN STEP ONE! LET'S JUMP RIGHT INTO YOUR WRITTEN EXPRESSIONS. WHAT DO YOU HOPE TO GAIN FROM THIS JOURNALING PROCESS?

_____
_____
_____
_____

YOU ARE AWESOME!

TAKE A MINUTE TO THINK ABOUT LAST WEEK, LAST MONTH OR LAST YEAR. WHAT WERE SOME CHALLENGING TIMES? WHAT WERE SOME BARRIERS YOU EXPERIENCED DUE TO THESE CHALLENGING TIMES?

_____
_____
_____
_____

CHOOSE TODAY TO BE PRODUCTIVE!

-S. Mara

THIS IS MY YEAR

THIS YEAR IS GOING TO BE A PRODUCTIVE YEAR! LET'S START LIGHT...LIST 4 GOALS FOR THIS YEAR.

_____

_____

_____

_____

_____

_____

_____

WHAT ARE THE NECESSARY STEPS TO REACH GOAL #1?

_____

_____

_____

_____

_____

_____

_____

THIS IS MY YEAR

WHAT ARE THE NECESSARY STEPS TO REACH GOAL #2?

_____
_____
_____
_____
_____

WHAT ARE THE NECESSARY STEPS TO REACH GOAL #3?

_____
_____
_____
_____
_____

WHAT ARE THE NECESSARY STEPS TO REACH GOAL #4?

_____
_____
_____
_____
_____

THIS IS MY YEAR

IN ORDER TO STAY ON TRACK TO REACH YOUR GOALS YOU MUST CUT BACK ON UNPRODUCTIVE TIME. LIST 4 DISTRACTIONS THAT ARE UNPRODUCTIVE. GET SPECIFIC!!
(Example: app usage, TV time, etc)

_____

_____

_____

_____

_____

_____

_____

_____

_____

_____

_____

_____

THIS IS MY YEAR

ACTION TIME!

THIS IS MY YEAR

ACTION TIME!
HOW WILL YOU CUT BACK ON DISTRACTION #1?
(example: only use the specific app before bed on the weekends, only watch tv at this certain time, etc.)

HOW WILL YOU CUT BACK ON DISTRACTION #2?
_____
_____
_____
_____

HOW WILL YOU CUT BACK ON DISTRACTION #3?
_____
_____
_____
_____

HOW WILL YOU CUT BACK ON DISTRACTION #4?
_____
_____
_____
_____

THIS IS MY YEAR

ESTABLISH BOUNDARIES FOR YOU CONTROL THE INPUT & OUTPUT THAT DRIVES YOUR DESTINY!

-S. Mara

SERENITY BREAK!!

TELL ME SOMETHING GOOD! WHAT ARE YOU GRATEFUL FOR?

_____

_____

_____

_____

_____

_____

_____

_____

_____

_____

_____

_____

_____

_____

_____

THIS IS MY YEAR

WHERE DO YOU FIND INSPIRATION? WHAT INSPIRES YOU?

THIS IS MY YEAR

BE INSPIRING!

-S. Mara

THIS IS MY YEAR

HOW CAN YOU BE INSPIRING TO OTHERS?

_____
_____
_____
_____
_____
_____
_____
_____
_____
_____
_____
_____
_____
_____
_____
_____
_____

THIS IS MY YEAR

ACTION TIME!
LET'S TRACK YOUR PROGRESS WEEKLY TOWARDS THE GOALS YOU LISTED ON PAGE 4!

Week Date: _____

THIS WEEK I FELT

_____
_____
_____

I WORKED TOWARDS MY GOALS BY

_____
_____
_____

WHAT DO YOU PLAN ON DOING NEXT WEEK TO WORK TOWARDS ACCOMPLISHING SET GOALS?

_____
_____
_____

THIS IS MY YEAR

Week Date: _____

THIS WEEK I FELT

_____
_____
_____

I WAS PRODUCTIVE TOWARDS MY GOALS BY

_____
_____

WHAT DO YOU PLAN ON DOING NEXT WEEK TO WORK TOWARDS ACCOMPLISHING SET GOALS?

_____
_____

I HAVE ACCOMPLISHED ATLEAST ONE OF MY GOALS.

YES OR NO

IF YES, WHICH GOAL WAS ACCOMPLISHED?

_____
_____

THIS IS MY YEAR

Week Date: _____

THIS WEEK I FELT

_____
_____
_____

I WORKED TOWARDS MY GOALS BY

_____
_____

WHAT DO YOU PLAN ON DOING NEXT WEEK TO WORK TOWARDS ACCOMPLISHING SET GOALS?

_____
_____

I HAVE ACCOMPLISHED ATLEAST ONE OF MY GOALS.

YES OR NO

IF YES, WHICH GOAL WAS ACCOMPLISHED?

_____
_____

THIS IS MY YEAR

KEEP GOING! YOU ARE JUST GETTING STARTED!

KEEP TRACKING YOUR PROGRESS WEEKLY!

THIS IS MY YEAR

Week Date: _____

THIS WEEK I FELT

_____

_____

_____

I WORKED TOWARDS MY GOALS BY

_____

_____

WHAT DO YOU PLAN ON DOING NEXT WEEK TO WORK TOWARDS ACCOMPLISHING SET GOALS?

_____

_____

I HAVE ACCOMPLISHED ATLEAST ONE OF MY GOALS.

YES OR NO

IF YES, WHICH GOAL WAS ACCOMPLISHED?

_____

_____

THIS IS MY YEAR

SERENITY BREAK!!

DESCRIBE IN DETAIL YOUR NEXT VACATION. WHERE WILL IT BE? WHO WILL GO WITH YOU? WHAT DO YOU WANT TO ACCOMPLISH ON THE VACATION?

_____
_____
_____
_____
_____
_____
_____
_____
_____
_____
_____
_____
_____
_____
_____
_____

THIS IS MY YEAR

Week Date: _____

THIS WEEK I FELT

_____

_____

_____

I WORKED TOWARDS MY GOALS BY

_____

_____

WHAT DO YOU PLAN ON DOING NEXT WEEK TO WORK TOWARDS ACCOMPLISHING SET GOALS?

_____

_____

I HAVE ACCOMPLISHED ATLEAST ONE OF MY GOALS.

YES OR NO

IF YES, WHICH GOAL WAS ACCOMPLISHED?

_____

_____

THIS IS MY YEAR

Week Date: _____

THIS WEEK I FELT

_____
_____
_____

I WORKED TOWARDS MY GOALS BY

_____
_____

WHAT DO YOU PLAN ON DOING NEXT WEEK TO WORK TOWARDS ACCOMPLISHING SET GOALS?

_____
_____

I HAVE ACCOMPLISHED ATLEAST ONE OF MY GOALS.

YES OR NO

IF YES, WHICH GOAL WAS ACCOMPLISHED?

_____
_____

THIS IS MY YEAR

Week Date: _____

THIS WEEK I FELT

_____

_____

_____

I WORKED TOWARDS MY GOALS BY

_____

_____

WHAT DO YOU PLAN ON DOING NEXT WEEK TO WORK TOWARDS ACCOMPLISHING SET GOALS?

_____

_____

I HAVE ACCOMPLISHED ATLEAST ONE OF MY GOALS.

YES OR NO

IF YES, WHICH GOAL WAS ACCOMPLISHED?

_____

_____

THIS IS MY YEAR

ALLOW YOURSELF TO BE HAPPY, GENUINELY HAPPY!

-S. Mara

THIS IS MY YEAR

Week Date: _____

THIS WEEK I FELT

_____
_____
_____

I WORKED TOWARDS MY GOALS BY

_____
_____

WHAT DO YOU PLAN ON DOING NEXT WEEK TO WORK TOWARDS ACCOMPLISHING SET GOALS?

_____
_____

I HAVE ACCOMPLISHED ATLEAST ONE OF MY GOALS.

YES OR NO

IF YES, WHICH GOAL WAS ACCOMPLISHED?

_____
_____

THIS IS MY YEAR

Week Date: _____

THIS WEEK I FELT

_____

_____

_____

I WORKED TOWARDS MY GOALS BY

_____

_____

WHAT DO YOU PLAN ON DOING NEXT WEEK TO WORK TOWARDS ACCOMPLISHING SET GOALS?

_____

_____

I HAVE ACCOMPLISHED ATLEAST ONE OF MY GOALS.

YES OR NO

IF YES, WHICH GOAL WAS ACCOMPLISHED?

_____

_____

THIS IS MY YEAR

SERENITY BREAK!!

LIST ALL OF THE POSITIVE WORDS THAT COME TO YOUR MIND IN THE NEXT 30 SECONDS!

_____
_____
_____
_____
_____
_____
_____
_____
_____
_____
_____
_____
_____
_____

THIS IS MY YEAR

Week Date: _____

THIS WEEK I FELT

_____
_____
_____

I WORKED TOWARDS MY GOALS BY

_____
_____

WHAT DO YOU PLAN ON DOING NEXT WEEK TO WORK TOWARDS ACCOMPLISHING SET GOALS?

_____
_____

I HAVE ACCOMPLISHED ATLEAST ONE OF MY GOALS.

YES OR NO

IF YES, WHICH GOAL WAS ACCOMPLISHED?

_____
_____

THIS IS MY YEAR

Week Date: _____

THIS WEEK I FELT

_____

_____

_____

I WORKED TOWARDS MY GOALS BY

_____

_____

WHAT DO YOU PLAN ON DOING NEXT WEEK TO WORK TOWARDS ACCOMPLISHING SET GOALS?

_____

_____

I HAVE ACCOMPLISHED ATLEAST ONE OF MY GOALS.

YES OR NO

IF YES, WHICH GOAL WAS ACCOMPLISHED?

_____

_____

THIS IS MY YEAR

Week Date: _____

THIS WEEK I FELT

_____
_____
_____

I WORKED TOWARDS MY GOALS BY

_____
_____

WHAT DO YOU PLAN ON DOING NEXT WEEK TO WORK TOWARDS ACCOMPLISHING SET GOALS?

_____
_____

I HAVE ACCOMPLISHED ATLEAST ONE OF MY GOALS.
YES OR NO

IF YES, WHICH GOAL WAS ACCOMPLISHED?

_____
_____

THIS IS MY YEAR

PUT POSITIVE THOUGHTS INTO YOUR EVERYDAY BEING!

-S. Mara

THIS IS MY YEAR

Week Date: _____

THIS WEEK I FELT

_____
_____
_____

I WORKED TOWARDS MY GOALS BY

_____
_____

WHAT DO YOU PLAN ON DOING NEXT WEEK TO WORK TOWARDS ACCOMPLISHING SET GOALS?

_____
_____

I HAVE ACCOMPLISHED ATLEAST ONE OF MY GOALS.
YES OR NO

IF YES, WHICH GOAL WAS ACCOMPLISHED?

_____
_____

THIS IS MY YEAR

Week Date: _____

THIS WEEK I FELT

_____
_____
_____

I WORKED TOWARDS MY GOALS BY

_____
_____

WHAT DO YOU PLAN ON DOING NEXT WEEK TO WORK TOWARDS ACCOMPLISHING SET GOALS?

_____
_____

I HAVE ACCOMPLISHED ATLEAST ONE OF MY GOALS.

YES OR NO

IF YES, WHICH GOAL WAS ACCOMPLISHED?

_____
_____

THIS IS MY YEAR

Week Date: _____

THIS WEEK I FELT

_____
_____
_____

I WORKED TOWARDS MY GOALS BY

_____
_____

WHAT DO YOU PLAN ON DOING NEXT WEEK TO WORK TOWARDS ACCOMPLISHING SET GOALS?

_____
_____

I HAVE ACCOMPLISHED ATLEAST ONE OF MY GOALS.

YES OR NO

IF YES, WHICH GOAL WAS ACCOMPLISHED?

_____
_____

THIS IS MY YEAR

Week Date: _____

THIS WEEK I FELT

_____
_____
_____

I WORKED TOWARDS MY GOALS BY

_____
_____

WHAT DO YOU PLAN ON DOING NEXT WEEK TO WORK TOWARDS ACCOMPLISHING SET GOALS?

_____
_____

I HAVE ACCOMPLISHED ATLEAST ONE OF MY GOALS.

YES OR NO

IF YES, WHICH GOAL WAS ACCOMPLISHED?

_____
_____

THIS IS MY YEAR

YOU HAVE THE HANG OF TRACKING YOUR PROGRESSION NOW! LET'S ADVANCE TO EVERY OTHER WEEK TRACKING!

-S. Mara

Week Date: _____

THE LAST TWO WEEKS I FELT

_____

_____

I WORKED TOWARDS MY GOALS BY

_____

_____

WHAT DO YOU PLAN ON DOING NEXT WEEK TO WORK TOWARDS ACCOMPLISHING SET GOALS?

_____

_____

I HAVE ACCOMPLISHED ATLEAST ONE OF MY GOALS.

YES OR NO

IF YES, WHICH GOAL WAS ACCOMPLISHED?

_____

_____

I HAVE A NEW GOAL I AM WORKING TOWARDS NOW

_____

_____

THIS IS MY YEAR

Week Date: _____

THE LAST TWO WEEKS I FELT

_____

_____

I WORKED TOWARDS MY GOALS BY

_____

_____

WHAT DO YOU PLAN ON DOING NEXT WEEK TO WORK TOWARDS ACCOMPLISHING SET GOALS?

_____

_____

I HAVE ACCOMPLISHED ATLEAST ONE OF MY GOALS.

YES OR NO

IF YES, WHICH GOAL WAS ACCOMPLISHED?

_____

_____

I HAVE A NEW GOAL I AM WORKING TOWARDS NOW

_____

_____

THIS IS MY YEAR

I ACCEPT ALL GOOD THINGS WITH GRATITUDE AND THE NEGATIVE AS LESSONS LEARNED.

-S. Mara

Week Date: _____

THE LAST TWO WEEKS I FELT

_____

_____

I WORKED TOWARDS MY GOALS BY

_____

_____

WHAT DO YOU PLAN ON DOING NEXT WEEK TO WORK TOWARDS ACCOMPLISHING SET GOALS?

_____

_____

I HAVE ACCOMPLISHED ATLEAST ONE OF MY GOALS.

YES OR NO

IF YES, WHICH GOAL WAS ACCOMPLISHED?

_____

_____

I HAVE A NEW GOAL I AM WORKING TOWARDS NOW

_____

_____

THIS IS MY YEAR

SERENITY BREAK!!

ACT OF KINDNESS CHALLENGE! THIS WEEK PERFORM TWO ACTS OF KINDNESS FOR OTHERS AND EXPRESS HOW IT MADE YOU FEEL.

_____
_____
_____
_____
_____
_____
_____
_____
_____
_____
_____
_____
_____
_____

THIS IS MY YEAR

Week Date: _____

THE LAST TWO WEEKS I FELT

_____

_____

I WORKED TOWARDS MY GOALS BY

_____

_____

WHAT DO YOU PLAN ON DOING NEXT WEEK TO WORK TOWARDS ACCOMPLISHING SET GOALS?

_____

_____

I HAVE ACCOMPLISHED ATLEAST ONE OF MY GOALS.

YES OR NO

IF YES, WHICH GOAL WAS ACCOMPLISHED?

_____

_____

I HAVE A NEW GOAL I AM WORKING TOWARDS NOW

_____

_____

THIS IS MY YEAR

I OWN MY JOURNEY!

-S. Mara

THIS IS MY YEAR

Week Date: _____

THE LAST TWO WEEKS I FELT

_____
_____

I WORKED TOWARDS MY GOALS BY

_____
_____

WHAT DO YOU PLAN ON DOING NEXT WEEK TO WORK TOWARDS ACCOMPLISHING SET GOALS?

_____
_____

I HAVE ACCOMPLISHED ATLEAST ONE OF MY GOALS.
YES OR NO

IF YES, WHICH GOAL WAS ACCOMPLISHED?

_____
_____

I HAVE A NEW GOAL I AM WORKING TOWARDS NOW

_____
_____

THIS IS MY YEAR

Week Date: _____

THE LAST TWO WEEKS I FELT
_____
_____

I WORKED TOWARDS MY GOALS BY
_____
_____

WHAT DO YOU PLAN ON DOING NEXT WEEK TO WORK TOWARDS ACCOMPLISHING SET GOALS?
_____
_____

I HAVE ACCOMPLISHED ATLEAST ONE OF MY GOALS.
YES OR NO

IF YES, WHICH GOAL WAS ACCOMPLISHED?
_____
_____

I HAVE A NEW GOAL I AM WORKING TOWARDS NOW
_____
_____

THIS IS MY YEAR

LET GO OF THE NEGATIVITY

&

GRASPS TIGHT TO POSITIVE ENERGY!

THIS IS MY YEAR

Week Date: _____

THE LAST TWO WEEKS I FELT

_____
_____

I WORKED TOWARDS MY GOALS BY

_____
_____

WHAT DO YOU PLAN ON DOING NEXT WEEK TO WORK TOWARDS ACCOMPLISHING SET GOALS?

_____
_____

I HAVE ACCOMPLISHED ATLEAST ONE OF MY GOALS.
YES OR NO

IF YES, WHICH GOAL WAS ACCOMPLISHED?

_____
_____

I HAVE A NEW GOAL I AM WORKING TOWARDS NOW

_____
_____

THIS IS MY YEAR

SERENITY BREAK!!

WHAT SONGS HELP YOU TO RELAX?

_____
_____
_____
_____
_____
_____
_____
_____
_____
_____
_____
_____
_____
_____
_____

THIS IS MY YEAR

Week Date: _____

THE LAST TWO WEEKS I FELT

_____

_____

I WORKED TOWARDS MY GOALS BY

_____

_____

WHAT DO YOU PLAN ON DOING NEXT WEEK TO WORK TOWARDS ACCOMPLISHING SET GOALS?

_____

_____

I HAVE ACCOMPLISHED ATLEAST ONE OF MY GOALS.

YES OR NO

IF YES, WHICH GOAL WAS ACCOMPLISHED?

_____

_____

I HAVE A NEW GOAL I AM WORKING TOWARDS NOW

_____

_____

THIS IS MY YEAR

WHAT YOU GIVE IS WHAT YOU GET!

-S. Mara

Week Date: _____

THE LAST TWO WEEKS I FELT

_____

_____

I WORKED TOWARDS MY GOALS BY

_____

_____

WHAT DO YOU PLAN ON DOING NEXT WEEK TO WORK TOWARDS ACCOMPLISHING SET GOALS?

_____

_____

I HAVE ACCOMPLISHED ATLEAST ONE OF MY GOALS.
YES OR NO

IF YES, WHICH GOAL WAS ACCOMPLISHED?

_____

_____

I HAVE A NEW GOAL I AM WORKING TOWARDS NOW

_____

_____

THIS IS MY YEAR

Week Date: _____

THE LAST TWO WEEKS I FELT
_____
_____

I WORKED TOWARDS MY GOALS BY
_____
_____

WHAT DO YOU PLAN ON DOING NEXT WEEK TO WORK TOWARDS ACCOMPLISHING SET GOALS?
_____
_____

I HAVE ACCOMPLISHED ATLEAST ONE OF MY GOALS.
YES OR NO

IF YES, WHICH GOAL WAS ACCOMPLISHED?
_____
_____

I HAVE A NEW GOAL I AM WORKING TOWARDS NOW
_____
_____

THIS IS MY YEAR

ALL IT TAKES IS ONE!

YOU ARE THAT ONE!

YOU'RE A LIFE CHANGER!

-S. Mara

THIS IS MY YEAR

Week Date: _____

THE LAST TWO WEEKS I FELT

_____

_____

I WORKED TOWARDS MY GOALS BY

_____

_____

WHAT DO YOU PLAN ON DOING NEXT WEEK TO WORK TOWARDS ACCOMPLISHING SET GOALS?

_____

_____

I HAVE ACCOMPLISHED ATLEAST ONE OF MY GOALS.

YES OR NO

IF YES, WHICH GOAL WAS ACCOMPLISHED?

_____

_____

I HAVE A NEW GOAL I AM WORKING TOWARDS NOW

_____

_____

THIS IS MY YEAR

SERENITY BREAK!!

WHAT WAS A TIME YOU FELT PURE HAPPINESS IN YOUR LIFE?

_____

_____

_____

_____

_____

_____

_____

_____

_____

_____

_____

_____

THIS IS MY YEAR

Week Date: _____

THE LAST TWO WEEKS I FELT
_____
_____

I WORKED TOWARDS MY GOALS BY
_____
_____

WHAT DO YOU PLAN ON DOING NEXT WEEK TO WORK TOWARDS ACCOMPLISHING SET GOALS?
_____
_____

I HAVE ACCOMPLISHED ATLEAST ONE OF MY GOALS.
YES OR NO

IF YES, WHICH GOAL WAS ACCOMPLISHED?
_____
_____

I HAVE A NEW GOAL I AM WORKING TOWARDS NOW
_____
_____

THIS IS MY YEAR

INVESTIN YOUR HAPPINESS!

-S. Mara

THIS IS MY YEAR

Week Date: _____

THE LAST TWO WEEKS I FELT

_____

_____

I WORKED TOWARDS MY GOALS BY

_____

_____

WHAT DO YOU PLAN ON DOING NEXT WEEK TO WORK TOWARDS ACCOMPLISHING SET GOALS?

_____

_____

I HAVE ACCOMPLISHED ATLEAST ONE OF MY GOALS.

YES OR NO

IF YES, WHICH GOAL WAS ACCOMPLISHED?

_____

_____

I HAVE A NEW GOAL I AM WORKING TOWARDS NOW

_____

_____

THIS IS MY YEAR

Week Date: _____

THE LAST TWO WEEKS I FELT

_____

_____

I WORKED TOWARDS MY GOALS BY

_____

_____

WHAT DO YOU PLAN ON DOING NEXT WEEK TO WORK TOWARDS ACCOMPLISHING SET GOALS?

_____

_____

I HAVE ACCOMPLISHED ATLEAST ONE OF MY GOALS.

YES OR NO

IF YES, WHICH GOAL WAS ACCOMPLISHED?

_____

_____

I HAVE A NEW GOAL I AM WORKING TOWARDS NOW

_____

_____

THIS IS MY YEAR

GIVE YOURSELF PERMISSION TO BE SUCCESSFUL!

-S. Mara

Week Date: _____

THE LAST TWO WEEKS I FELT

_____

_____

I WORKED TOWARDS MY GOALS BY

_____

_____

WHAT DO YOU PLAN ON DOING NEXT WEEK TO WORK TOWARDS ACCOMPLISHING SET GOALS?

_____

_____

I HAVE ACCOMPLISHED ATLEAST ONE OF MY GOALS.

YES OR NO

IF YES, WHICH GOAL WAS ACCOMPLISHED?

_____

_____

I HAVE A NEW GOAL I AM WORKING TOWARDS NOW

_____

_____

THIS IS MY YEAR

SERENITY BREAK!!

CLOSE YOUR EYES AND GO TO YOUR HAPPY PLACE! STAY THERE FOR TWO MINUTES.

_____
_____
_____
_____
_____
_____
_____
_____
_____
_____
_____
_____
_____
_____

THIS IS MY YEAR

Week Date: _____

THE LAST TWO WEEKS I FELT

_____

_____

I WORKED TOWARDS MY GOALS BY

_____

_____

WHAT DO YOU PLAN ON DOING NEXT WEEK TO WORK TOWARDS ACCOMPLISHING SET GOALS?

_____

_____

I HAVE ACCOMPLISHED ATLEAST ONE OF MY GOALS.

YES OR NO

IF YES, WHICH GOAL WAS ACCOMPLISHED?

_____

_____

I HAVE A NEW GOAL I AM WORKING TOWARDS NOW

_____

_____

THIS IS MY YEAR

YOU ARE ENOUGH!

-S. Mara

THIS IS MY YEAR

Week Date: _____

THE LAST TWO WEEKS I FELT

_____

_____

I WORKED TOWARDS MY GOALS BY

_____

_____

WHAT DO YOU PLAN ON DOING NEXT WEEK TO WORK TOWARDS ACCOMPLISHING SET GOALS?

_____

_____

I HAVE ACCOMPLISHED ATLEAST ONE OF MY GOALS.

YES OR NO

IF YES, WHICH GOAL WAS ACCOMPLISHED?

_____

_____

I HAVE A NEW GOAL I AM WORKING TOWARDS NOW

_____

_____

THIS IS MY YEAR

Week Date: _____

THE LAST TWO WEEKS I FELT

_____

_____

I WORKED TOWARDS MY GOALS BY

_____

_____

WHAT DO YOU PLAN ON DOING NEXT WEEK TO WORK TOWARDS ACCOMPLISHING SET GOALS?

_____

_____

I HAVE ACCOMPLISHED ATLEAST ONE OF MY GOALS.

YES OR NO

IF YES, WHICH GOAL WAS ACCOMPLISHED?

_____

_____

I HAVE A NEW GOAL I AM WORKING TOWARDS NOW

_____

_____

THIS IS MY YEAR

Week Date: _____

THE LAST TWO WEEKS I FELT
_____
_____

I WORKED TOWARDS MY GOALS BY
_____
_____

WHAT DO YOU PLAN ON DOING NEXT WEEK TO WORK TOWARDS ACCOMPLISHING SET GOALS?
_____
_____

I HAVE ACCOMPLISHED ATLEAST ONE OF MY GOALS.
YES OR NO

IF YES, WHICH GOAL WAS ACCOMPLISHED?
_____
_____

I HAVE A NEW GOAL I AM WORKING TOWARDS NOW
_____
_____

THIS IS MY YEAR

IT'S BEEN A WHOLE 52 WEEKS OF JOURNALING! HOPEFULLY ONE OR TWO OF YOUR GOALS HAVE BEEN ACCOMPLISHED!

THIS IS MY YEAR

YOU ARE CAPABLE OF ACCOMPLISHING WHATEVER GOAL YOU SET. YOU HAVE SHOWN DISCIPLINE, MOTIVATION AND ACCOUNTABILITY IN THIS JOURNAL PROCESS!

"THIS IS MY YEAR"

-S. Mara

www.ingramcontent.com/pod-product-compliance
Lightning Source LLC
Chambersburg PA
CBHW070849160426
43192CB00012B/2374